Death and Letting Go

ELLEN TADD

MONTAGUE
PRESS

Published by Montague Press, P.O. Box B-11
Montague, Massachusetts 01351

Library of Congress Control Number: 2002111210
ISBN 1-932151-00-1

Publisher's Cataloging-in-Publication
(Provided by Quality Books, Inc.)

Tadd, Ellen.
    Death and letting go / Ellen Tadd.
    p. cm.
    LCCN 2002111210
    ISBN 1-932151-00-1

    1. Death--Psychological aspects. 2. Bereavement--Psychological aspects. 3. Spiritualism. 4. Future life   I. Title

BF789.D4T34 2003   155.9'37
                                              QB133-863

To Martha Miller

FOREWORD

M Y WIFE MARGIE AND I CAME TO
California in 1976. In San Diego we started
our own full-service leadership training and
consulting firm, and now have 240 people working
with us in the United States, with partners in thirty
nations around the world.

Since moving to California, I have learned not
to discount anything. This state is a great melting pot
of cultures and ideas as diverse as its geography,
ranging from deserts and valleys to mountains and
wonderful beaches. This diversity is a reflection of
the endless worlds of new ideas and thoughts waiting
to be explored by the people who live here.

When I listen to Ellen's stories, that California
spirit kicks in. I had the pleasure of meeting this
unique woman through a good friend, who
introduced me to Ellen several years ago. What I
found when we first got together was a caring and
loving person who has some remarkable insights and

an understanding of the past and future that I had never thought about in my own journeys.

For example, one time I asked Ellen about my sister Sandy. I didn't tell her Sandy had died, but Ellen immediately knew what the circumstances were. She had incredible insights about my sister's past life and present. She told me that Sandy was still in turmoil and consumed by issues she had not resolved. Ellen told me that my mother and I could communicate with Sandy and help her by speaking to her directly. After the difficult task of explaining what a clairvoyant was to my mother, she was thrilled and so was I.

Based on many personal stories from Ellen's past, *Death and Letting Go* can be used as an important entry into talking about this difficult subject – one we all must face. What she says about death and dying is very helpful, no matter what your faith or religion. Ellen's book not only encourages us to deal with death now, but also helps us consider how we live day in and day out too. It did for me.

So, as I am thankful for the wonderfully rich

and diverse state I now call home, I am also thankful for people like Ellen. Thank you, Ellen for being who you are. Your wonderful wisdom and insights are a blessing to my life. I think this is a book that everyone should read and benefit from.

KEN BLANCHARD
co-author of *The One Minute Manager*

CONTENTS

INTRODUCTION

*T*HE PURPOSE OF THIS BOOK IS TO reveal to some and remind others that death is a continuation of life. As part of the experience of life for all beings, death is simply a door into another realm. In our culture, death is commonly viewed as an ending, rather than as a completion of one phase and the entering into a new chapter of existence. The awareness that death is not an end allows for greater enjoyment of the entire process of life, including the transition into the spiritual world.

I became convinced that death is a

continuation of life when my mother came back and spoke to me after she died. This unique experience happened just after I completed my freshman year of college and was visiting my brother in New York City. There I met his new girlfriend Catherine, an aspiring actress, who also turned out to be a gifted trance medium. At the time, however, I was uncertain whether "mediumship" was genuine.

In my first conversation with Catherine, I remember being startled when she asked me if there was anyone who was dead that I would like to speak with. Despite my surprise, I knew immediately that I wanted to speak with my mother, if possible. My mother had a difficult life. She suffered with crippling multiple sclerosis, which affected both her mind and body. My mother first became ill when I was two years old and as a result, I had known her primarily as a sick person. As her child I suffered with her, feeling helpless to heal her or understand why this terrible tragedy happened to our family. So when it was suggested that I could communicate with her in spiritual form, even though I was skeptical, I was excited by the opportunity to try.

My skepticism soon vanished as I watched Catherine enter into a trance state. While going into trance, she had to lie down, taking on my mother's former physical state of paralysis. I could see my mother's features clearly superimposed over the medium's face. Witnessing this dramatic process, I became totally convinced that people of a certain sensitivity can act as intermediaries contacting those in spiritual realms, and that there is life after death.

With great effort, my mother spoke to me. She explained that she had chosen a life of difficulty to learn compassion for those who suffer and that no matter how things appear on the surface, if you look deep enough, you will see that there is always justice. Listening to her, I began to comprehend an intricate, interconnected process of lessons which affect everyone. My mother's presence and message healed my childhood trauma and transformed my view of the world. It also reopened the clairvoyant and clairaudient gifts that I'd had as a child, but had repressed out of fear that something was wrong with me.

It amazed me that this experience took place in Manhattan, since I had always lived in the country and felt more comfortable there. But New York offered me the opportunity to walk through enormous crowds. As I looked into peoples' eyes, I saw for the first time that all people were Spirit and they were infinite. I recognized that most people did not know who they were or why they were here. I became aware that part of my purpose on the earth was to help others remember their spiritual identity and identify their purpose. Very soon after this awakening, I began to have contact with guides from spiritual realms and discovered that I could serve as an intermediary between the material and spiritual worlds.

My first encounter with a guide happened just after I'd had a severe case of the flu. I believe my weakened condition prepared me to just be open to the experience and not analyze it. I awoke from a deep sleep at three in the morning. Over my bed, floating in the air above me was a Chinese man's face, of scintillating light. This was not a dream – I was completely awake. Although I was startled, the purity and compassion emanating from his face put me immediately at ease. I knew I could absolutely trust him. In this initial connection, no ideas were shared; I just felt his illumined presence. Later, he would periodically appear to me, telepathically teaching about the meaning of spiritual principles.

Since that first contact, I've had the privilege of communicating with many individuals in spiritual form. From these experiences I've gathered information, both philosophical and practical. I've received profound teachings from wise and compassionate guides. I have also had the opportunity to clairvoyantly observe the multidimensional life process of birth and death, as individuals move between the material and spiritual realms.

This book is a collection of stories based on these personal and clairvoyant experiences. It also includes reports from students about their encounters. The stories I have chosen illustrate basic principles and tools that can universally be applied in death or any time of transition.

Death is an inevitable fate that everyone must face. Still, the topic of death is often avoided or denied because of fears and misunderstandings about what death actually is. When we recognize death as a continuation of life, we release fears that prevent a fuller experience of material existence.

Just as attitudes and actions in one's material life affect the quality of that life, the attitudes and actions after death affect the quality of life in the next realm. As individuals become more conscious and responsible for the thoughts and focus they choose, they can have a greater impact on the quality and circumstances in life and after death. By addressing fears and attachments all throughout one's life, the death process simply becomes a continuation of this same lesson and life-long practice of letting go.

There are many different types of death experiences. These mirror the attachments, fears, and aspirations of each individual. When leaving the physical body, aspiring to spiritual qualities such as compassion, forgiveness, or truth propels an individual into an expansive force of light and ecstasy. On the other hand, if a person is immersed in fear, regret, guilt, or disappointment, he or she may become anchored in density after death. This can manifest as being "earth-bound" (caught in earth experiences while in spiritual form), or becoming trapped in limited or "lower vibrational" realms, which are restrictive and confining. Such experiences can last for a long period of time. Unfortunately, it is difficult for guides in spiritual dimensions to help these people because guides are unable to usurp free will and enter the density caused by negative attitudes. Therefore, earth-bound or confined individuals stuck in lower realms must let go of attachments to the past and focus on positive thoughts and feelings in order for guides and helpers to reach them.

When letting go occurs in the after-death state, an expansion of consciousness and an energetic lightness develops in the non-physical body. This feels and appears to me like a balloon that has been trapped and freed to rise up into the higher spheres. Access to enlightened individuals who reside in these higher realms then becomes available. These beings offer comfort and insight about the last life on earth, as well as teaching attitudes favorable for spiritual growth and personal fulfillment in future lives.

I have come to recognize that people's experiences after death are as varied as their experiences in the physical world. It has been fascinating to study through clairvoyance the attitudes and circumstances involved in a desirable death versus a painful and confused one. My hope is that this book will help people move through fears and apprehensions surrounding death which inhibit enjoyment of life on earth and quality of life after death. Also, I will provide information that can prevent people from becoming trapped in lower realms, once life in the material world has been completed. Finally, I wish to communicate to loved ones left behind, that relationships do not end because we die. Love, support, and ideas can be exchanged between individuals in the physical and spiritual realms.

We all must address this topic at one stage or another in our lives, whether through the death of a loved one, helping a friend accept a death in their family, or confronting our own time to leave the body. My experiences have taught me that knowledge about death can dissipate fear and aid in a successful passing into the spiritual world. At the time of death, a comfortable, illumined, and expansive transition from one life to the next is available to everyone.

CHAPTER ONE: Death and Birth

R ECENTLY, AN INDIVIDUAL CAME TO speak to me from the spiritual dimension about his experiences in a lifetime as a Native American. During that time, he lived in a culture in which death and transition were integrated into the rituals and consciousness of daily life. He said:

When I walked the earth, the earth was a place of great beauty. There was not the pollution, nor the lack of care to the world that is a part of your world today. As I walked through the trees, I knew that the gift of sunlight was precious. I knew that the gift of the air that I breathed should not be taken for granted. I knew that the rain was nourishing all of life including me. And so I was in harmony. I was in harmony with all of the parts of nature, and it made it easier for me to trust that life and death were a natural cycle, because I observed it all around me. I observed it in the plants. I observed it in the animals, and I was close to it in my tribe and with my people.

Death was not hidden away as it is hidden in your culture. But it was something that we looked upon every day as a part of life. The animals that we ate, we were a part of killing them. We were a part of cutting them. We were a part of eating them with the knowledge of the whole process of sacrifice that was necessary to bring life to our people. And when a person died who was near and dear to us, they were brought out for the public to see. They were brought out to be acknowledged, to be mourned for, and to be honored as they entered into the spiritual realm. And so it is important once again for death not to be hidden away, but for death to be brought out, to be seen, to be not afraid of. And in that way, it shall be more easily embraced as a part of life, which is always close.

My experiences surrounding the incarnation and birth of my second child illustrate many principles involved in the transition between the material and spiritual worlds. My initial contact with the entity that would become my son took place after I learned I was pregnant. I already had one child but wanted an opportunity to develop my work before having another. For this reason, the discovery of my pregnancy produced anxiety and disappointment.

I knew it was possible to communicate through thought to individuals in spiritual realms, so I decided to call this entity to me. It was not long before my future son appeared to me in his spiritual body. He did not appear as a baby, but as a grown man, tall and handsome. His spiritual form had detailed features just like a physical body – bright blue eyes, brown hair, and a chiseled face, but it was all made of scintillating light.

I explained to him that I did want him to be born and that I would love him. I expressed out loud that my feelings of disappointment were not a rejection of him, but rather a recognition of poor timing. He communicated telepathically that he would leave and return at a time when it was more conducive to celebrate his arrival in the material world. When I woke up the next morning, I discovered that I had miscarried and felt tremendous relief and gratitude to my future son for his sensitivity and respect for my feelings.

As awareness grows that children are spiritual entities who exist prior to birth, the possibility of communicating with them becomes a practical reality. In certain cases, this communication can be a tool to determine the appropriateness of terminating a pregnancy and can facilitate a natural miscarriage. Clairvoyantly, I have observed a cord of energy connecting an entity with a fetus at the time of conception. However, I have never seen the actual entrance of a spirit into the body before the fourth month.

The recognition that an entity enters only after the fourth month and that the consciousness of the child continues to exist in another form can help to alleviate guilty feelings generated by a miscarriage or the voluntary termination of a pregnancy.

In my personal experience with my son, the natural miscarriage as a result of communication with him gave me a gift of time. I utilized the next six months to accomplish specific goals, and then I communicated to him in thought that he was now welcome. Soon afterwards, I became pregnant again, but this time I felt happy and prepared.

As my pregnancy progressed, I became aware that the spirit of my child was not around me. At my childbirth classes all the expectant mothers had spirits over their shoulders, but not me. In my previous pregnancy with my daughter, I had experienced her presence as a companion who walked with me through the developing time of the fetus. The absence of my son's presence frequently alarmed me, causing me to wonder if he would be healthy or stillborn. As my anxiety grew, he again came and comforted me, telepathically communicating that he was fine. He expressed the thought that he had more interesting and important things to do than to spend time with an expectant mother waiting to give birth.

The relationship with individual entities in spiritual form can be as varied as relationships with people in physical bodies. My clairvoyant experiences accurately revealed the differences between my two children's personalities. My daughter's nature is still one which seeks community and companionship, while my son is more active and self-reliant.

At the beginning of my labor, the spirit of my future son again appeared to me. This time he had a male guide on each side of him. All three of them were illumined by golden, glowing light. In thought he said to me, "I've come to see if you are all right." When I assured him that I was, the three of them left.

In the car on the way to the hospital, he manifested in his spiritual form for the last time. In this instance, he seemed about a foot tall. I learned from this experience that size is not fixed in the spiritual dimensions – an individual can manifest as large or small. As I watched him, his form began to dissolve, simultaneously from the top of his head and from the bottom of his feet, until only a beam of white light was left. This light then entered into the body of the new child. In a few hours, Misha was born.

After Misha's birth, I was overwhelmed with the feeling that the courage to be born was as great as the courage to die. Here was an individual who sacrificed his freedom and gave up the ability to travel and communicate with thought in order to enter the physical world. After birth, he became completely dependent on the people around him for sensitivity to all his needs. He had to acquire elementary abilities, such as walking, talking, and feeding himself.

These are humbling experiences we have all endured.

The awareness of existence prior to birth and the appreciation of the long journey to adulthood can help parents and children to be patient and compassionate with the frustrations of childhood development.

Another lesson I learned from this experience is that every child is truly his or her individual self, and not just an extension of their parents. While I helped create a physical form for this spiritual entity to enter into material life, his consciousness and tendencies existed before he entered the body. Each of us has unique lessons and purposes, but all of us have shared the journey from the spiritual to the material world.

Children have been in the physical realm for the shortest period of time. Therefore, their connection with the spiritual world is strong and it is not uncommon for them to see and converse with beings in spiritual form. These beings can be guides and helpers, play friends, or lost and confused individuals. Reassuring children that their ethereal encounters are natural can prevent them from becoming afraid.

A friend once told me when he was a child he would get frustrated and angry because his spirit friends could run up a tree and he couldn't. And in a meditation class with me, Susan told the story of how her two year old daughter saw spiritual beings as they drove past a graveyard. Her daughter Sara asked, " Why are there so many people standing around in the graveyard?" Her mother could not see them, but was wise enough to know that her child would have an easier time perceiving the spirit world.

At age two, my daughter had a spirit play friend. Our family never called her imaginary, because clairvoyantly I could see she was a little Japanese girl in her spirit body. Laura called her companion Hanna Peach. They played together over a period of months and gradually Hanna Peach stopped coming as Laura continued to grow older. Laura had many clairvoyant occurrences until she started school. I believe she shut down her ability to see into the spiritual realm because she feared seeming odd and wanted to be accepted by her peers. Spiritual experiences are not infrequent for children. With adult support and encouragement their metaphysical gifts are more likely to endure into their maturity, which in turn would help alleviate fears about death.

CHAPTER TWO: Images and Attitudes Go with You

*A*S INDIVIDUALS MOVE FROM THE material realm into the spiritual one, they carry attitudes, feelings, and images with them. These mental and emotional constructs, developed through a lifetime in the material world, can affect the quality of experience after death.

The truth of this was brought home to me when my mother came back and spoke to me after she had died. Prior to this experience, I had only questions about life after death, but no answers. I had assumed however, that if life did continue, a sick person would automatically become healthy in the after-death state. I was surprised to learn that even though my mother had dropped her body, she still had not recovered from a diseased condition.

Following the initial contact with my mother, I started to have regular communication with her on my own without an intermediary. She had been sick for so many of her adult years that she continued to hold the image of herself as an ill person, even though she was no longer in a physical body. Through telepathic communication and mental imagery, I was able to assist her in changing the way she perceived and manifested herself in the spiritual realm. To help me visualize and project positive images to her, I used a photograph of my mother as a young, beautiful, and healthy woman. At times I spoke out loud to her, telling her that she had been sick long enough and that now she could return to health and happiness.

Over a six-month period, I was able clairvoyantly to perceive the changes in my mother's appearance in the spiritual form, as well as in her state of mind. Her sad and diseased face was transformed, becoming young and radiant. Even her hair in spirit form shifted from black mixed with gray to completely black. Through this process, I learned that by helping her change her images and ideas of herself, she could once again become healthy and happy.

My mother's story illustrates that death does not always yield liberation or freedom from difficult life circumstances. But her story also dramatizes how communication and visualization can help people in spiritual form move out of fears and limited perceptions that trap them, keeping them stuck and struggling.

While most individuals do not have a developed clairvoyant gift, many people are able to sense the condition of loved ones who have passed into the next dimension of life. For others it may be more difficult. Still, it is always helpful to hold the image of loved ones who have died as vibrant, healthy, and at their best. This effort is never wasted. When we focus and send positive imagery to individuals after death, it helps them let go of the past and proceed to life's next phase. Photographs depicting positive qualities can be used as an aid in this process.

The belief that it is not possible to communicate and feel connected with individuals in spiritual form has caused much pain and suffering. It is never too late – even after a person has died – to express thoughts or feelings to resolve old circumstances and create a sense of support and interconnectedness. In the spiritual realms, thought and energy exchange are the medium of communication. Therefore, when focused thoughts and feelings are directed to an individual in spiritual form, they are received to varying degrees depending on the consciousness and location of the entity.

These concepts were experienced by my student Kelly and are relayed in her own story:

It was about six months after my sister Tracy died when a tremendous sense of sadness seemed to settle in around me. No matter which way I turned, I could not seem to lift it. I had been working with Ellen Tadd for a number of years before Tracy died, learning to live my life from a deeper spiritual perspective. Because of this work, I had been able to walk through my sister's seven months of illness and her death with a sense of certainty and peacefulness. So I was surprised by my sadness and I felt powerless to change it.

When Ellen tuned into Tracy, she could see that she had become stuck in her process of moving on from the physical world. Because the bond between us as sisters was so close and because I'd had such a strong hand in helping Tracy in the dying process, I had also become stuck. I believe my sadness was a symptom of this.

Ellen saw that Tracy had come to the point in her spiritual transformation where she was looking back over her life. In doing this, she was also assessing the times when she had made mistakes. My sister was feeling guilty and sad about the effects her mistakes had upon the people she loved. Ellen informed me that it was this dynamic of guilt and sadness that was holding both Tracy and me back in our letting go process. My sister was not seeing how her mistakes had been a necessary part of her learning and growing and I was not moving through the experience of her death to capture renewed life.

The recommendation Ellen gave was for me to begin a dialogue with Tracy to tell her about her mistakes that I remembered and to speak of them in stories that were helpful for her growth. She also recommended that I tell her my own stories that were continuing to unfold seemingly as mistakes, but truthfully as deeper learnings. It was important for Tracy to see mistakes as part of the human condition. If I could show her how I continued to integrate my own mistakes as learnings, she would in turn accept her own and be able to move on.

Ellen's advice rang true for me. I knew that all Tracy's years of confidence and determination also held an element of not wanting to make a mistake. I instantly felt empowered to once again be a part of *assisting Tracy to let go as I had in the seven months leading up to her death. I talked to my sister when I was alone and wrote to her in my journals. A few days after I began communicating with Tracy, my sadness was released. It was not a gradual sense of lifting, but an immediate one. I became aware that our bond and connection as sisters exists far beyond the human world.*

Some individuals who have passed into the spiritual realm hover around loved ones and familiar settings, while others go into what I have always termed "the morgue of healing." This appears to me like a very narrow resting-place of light for the purpose of healing and rejuvenation after a life of disease or difficulty. Others may seem out of reach and distant because they have moved into outer realms, far from the density of the material world. Here, guides and teachers direct them towards a continuation of growth and learning. Even after an individual has gone into the light and expansion of the outer realms, it is not uncommon for them to periodically visit to communicate, connect, and reassure. No matter which experience an individual gravitates towards after-death, it is important for loved ones left behind to release anxieties about this next stage of life so they can provide support.

For an individual to go into an expanded state after death, it is necessary to let go of the past and forgive people, situations, or oneself. When my mother spoke to me through the trance medium, she was able to forgive me for my lack of awareness and sensitivity to her struggle while she was alive, because she acknowledged that I had been a child. However, she had not forgiven my father for emotionally abandoning her after she became ill. By detaching from her, he attempted to protect himself from the pain of losing the woman he loved.

My mother remained unhappy and trapped until she accepted that everyone in her life had done the best they could given their limited awareness. For many people, including my father, fear blocks clarity and the ability to take appropriate action. As my mother began to heal, she came to recognize my father as an individual who was caught in fear and who was working through lessons in his own life. Then she was able to stop judging him, and could find forgiveness and personal liberation.

Liberation in the spiritual dimension comes from accessing universal spiritual qualities such as love, forgiveness, compassion, and truth. The specific principle or attitude that works as a key to release a feeling of confinement after death can vary from one individual to the next. An emphasis on trust can serve to antidote fears, while forgiveness, as in the case of my mother, heals hurts from the past. In another situation, a focus on creativity might address feelings of inadequacy that were inhibiting throughout a life.

Once my mother's self-image changed and she developed an acceptance and forgiveness of the past, she could then go on to the next phase and review her most recent life in the material world. The purpose of this life review was to gather information and insight concerning the lessons she had learned, what lessons she was working on and how to plan her next incarnation.

It is not necessary or even advisable to wait until death to reflect on past circumstances. In fact, it is extremely important to review thoughts, feelings, and images in the midst of one's life in order to take full advantage of the learning process. Reviewing life circumstances on an ongoing basis facilitates a state of conscious growth. This review also supports a fuller experience of life, a successful transition into death, and an improved state of being after death.

Recently I worked with a client whose sister Sally had just died of cancer. Throughout her life, Sally had not held a spiritual perspective and was not particularly self-reflective. I was curious about her dying process and her transition into spirit, and so I began by looking clairvoyantly into this woman's state of mind before she died. What I discovered was that Sally felt very angry about her circumstance, frightened about leaving her family, and fearful about the unknown. She was really in quite a panicked state. These attitudes can remain with an individual entering the spiritual realm and create distress and isolation there.

As I continued to project my consciousness into Sally, I became aware that a quick and radical change had occurred within her emotional state. This shift appeared to be connected with the effects of a painkiller. Her sister confirmed that Sally had been put on morphine at the very end of her life. It seemed to me that the introduction of this drug into her system created relaxation, and allowed her to feel acceptance, not resistance. When the time came for her spirit to leave her body, her consciousness was not focused on fear but on the spiritual attitude of acceptance. This allowed her to move quickly into positivity and light so guides and helpers could comfort and prepare her for the next stage of learning in the non-physical world.

Sally's story dramatizes that the use of drugs to alleviate pain and suffering at the end of one's life can also aid in a positive transition into the spiritual world. This does not negate the importance of attending to fears and working through limited attitudes while alive on the earth. If issues and lessons are not resolved, they will need to be attended to in the next realm and in future incarnations.

Recently, a lost entity who had no preparation for death contacted me for help. When I awoke in the middle of the night, above my bed was a man in spirit form. Just his head and torso were visible to me. His chest was bare and his eyes looked frightened and almost desperate for help. The self-image he brought into the spiritual realm was dirty and disheveled. His blond hair looked matted, as if it hadn't been washed in months, and his skin tone was ruddy, like a heavy drinker's. Intuitively, I felt he had been a homeless person who had died and didn't know where he was, or that he was dead. His self-image and attitudes went with him into the non-physical world. I was pleased that his appearance didn't startle or frighten me. After so many years of these types of experiences, I am no longer alarmed when a person in spiritual form comes into my sight.

I knew I could comfort him by sending him reassuring thoughts and images. Within only five minutes of my intense focus, his fears were soothed and his attitudes elevated. Then a helper from the spiritual realm came to contact him. The male guide's kind face and short brown hair were not distinct, but his presence felt reassuring and safe. I could hear him explain to the lost man that he had died and was now in the spirit world. In a moment they were gone.

There are many different types of death scenarios, yet it is always important to create a positive spiritual climate at the time of death. This can be achieved by communicating that everyone is spirit; that our identities will continue; that loved ones often welcome us in the next realm; and that guides and teachers will help us learn. If direct conversation is not possible, silent prayer or positive visualization will help generate positivity so guides and teachers can be reached.

CHAPTER THREE: Grief and Letting Go

WHEN MY DAUGHTER LAURA WAS ten years old, a dog she loved named Adam died unexpectedly. She became extremely upset, grieving and crying about him, and had difficulty accepting his death. A few weeks later Laura had an out-of-body experience in which she visited with Adam.

This occurred at a time when we were riding in the car and were both extremely tired. I put on some soothing music and suggested to Laura that she lie down in the back of the car for a rest. After a twenty-minute period, she sat up and explained that something wonderful had happened. She had left her body and gone into the spiritual realm to talk with her friend, Adam the dog.

During the out-of-body experience, Laura was able to communicate with Adam telepathically. He told her not to be unhappy that he left his body, and that her emotional turmoil was making it difficult for him. He said that if she really wanted to help him, what she should do was to send him her love and light, because that would support him on his new journey.

Adam also spoke to Laura in thought about her future, saying, "The reason I've come and talked with you is so that when someone closer to you dies, you will know what to do." Laura's emotional reaction to Adam's death dramatically changed after this experience. I knew her story was genuine. She even contacted Adam's owners to tell them of her experience and to inform them that Adam's self-image in the spirit world was groomed and not shaggy.

Very soon after this experience, my brother's wife gave birth to a baby boy. He was born with a terminal disease and only lived for eight weeks. During a hospital visit, Laura held her dying cousin. As Adam had advised, she focused on sending the baby love and light to ease his way out of the physical form.

Culturally, we have been taught that it is appropriate to feel grief-stricken and unhappy when someone dies. However, my guides teach that when there is a death, it is best to send thoughts of encouragement for continued growth and celebration for the liberation from the limitations of physical existence. It is not easy to make the shift to a new way of looking at death. Our conditioning is deep, and the concepts of letting go and trusting the natural cycles of life are not prevalent in our culture. However, what are now considered normal reactions to death will change, for human nature is evolving as individuals incorporate greater spiritual awareness into their daily lives.

With clairvoyant ability to see the spirit body, any doubt about the continuation of an individual after death is eliminated. I experienced this comfort when our dog Mittens died. He was part Collie, part St. Bernard, and part Golden Retriever, though sometimes he appeared more like a she-lion.

While following a neighbor across a major highway, Mittens was struck by a car and killed instantly. I reacted with shock and grief. However, it wasn't long before I noticed him in spiritual form, on the front porch in his favorite spot. He was still with us and I could see him. I couldn't hug him or feel his fur. Our relationship was changed, but I discovered that the love between us still existed. By focusing on our spiritual bond, I experienced contentment and appreciation for our time together and was able to let him go.

Carolyn, a student who had the experience of clairvoyantly seeing the spirit body and who no longer has doubts that there is a continuation of life after death, tells this story:

After my husband's death, I was drawn to hospice work because I felt I could support others as they were dying. One of my earliest hospice assignments left a lasting impression on me. It was the first time I was with someone when they died.

One afternoon the phone rang and it was Irene at hospice. "We have an emergency," she said. This time it was a woman in her 90s who needed to be attended to as she was not expected to live through the night. Later that evening I drove to the nursing home. While in my truck, I tried to focus myself and ask in thought, "What am I to do for this person?" Moments later I experienced a reply. The reply came in the form of an impression which said that I was to hold her in gold light. Deep within I knew this was my answer.

When I arrived in her room I pulled a chair next to Jane's bedside and was eager to visualize surrounding her in light. Initially, I could feel that Jane was tense. After a while, her breathing became much less labored. Continuing to use light I noticed that my breathing became synchronized with hers. Here was a woman I had not seen before and yet I began to feel a deep connection to her. The in and out of each breath led me to experience the present so deeply I felt a unity with Jane and momentarily lost the sense of feeling separate. In the midst of this, one of the nursing staff entered the room to check on her. Then two more staff members came in. I continued to watch Jane and focus on the connection we had established.

As one staff member cradled Jane's head and shoulders, the others attended to her. It was at this moment I experienced Jane's spirit leaving her body. As her spirit began leaving her face changed color. I saw a vibrating light at her feet which began moving upward. I said to the nurse, "She's leaving! She's leaving!" The nurse reached for her stethoscope and by the time she put it to the woman's chest, I had seen the woman's spirit go up and out the top of her head. Yes, Jane did leave but not without sharing a wonderful experience. I felt no fear from her as she departed, just a loving presence.

For me this verified what Ellen and her guides had been teaching us, that we are spirit. Thereafter, whenever I was with a hospice patient I saw them as spirit and not just the physical form, regardless of the condition of the body. I was able to hold the fact that they were spirit because I had seen it. I think it helped me in my daily life as I began to see everyone as spirit. This has changed how I view life and death.

When those left behind in the material world accept death as another stage of personal development, then focus can be placed on sending well wishes and love to the person or animal who has died. After death, individuals are often ready to let go and enter into the next realm of illumination and learning, but they may be held back due to concern for anguished and frightened loved ones. A supportive release helps to alleviate the feelings of trauma, fear, or guilt which often contribute to keeping the individual newly-arrived in the spiritual dimensions from going on into light and expansion.

The experience of a woman I counseled for many years provides an example of how attitudes and images held by family and friends impact individuals who have died. Her son and his friend were both killed in a car accident. The difference in the death experiences of these two young men was quite extreme because of their childhood conditioning and family response.

Because of his mother's influence, my client's son had basic information about life after death and believed that his true identity was spiritual and not physical. This awareness helped him to accept the situation more easily than his friend. There was sadness and grief that his life on earth was cut short, but there was also the knowledge that he would continue to grow, develop, and actualize his potential. His family members and friends gathered soon after his death to send a group message of love, light, prayer, and acceptance to him. This unified effort helped him to accept the radical change in his circumstance. He then was able to express his love to family and friends, and go on into light to be greeted and taught by spiritual guides who ushered him into his next chapter of life review.

Initially both families were filled with grief, shock, and disbelief. My student, Katja, described this in her own words:

When the policeman came to tell me the news of my son Julian and his friend's death in a car accident far away, I felt my vital energy flow out of my feet. I became incapable of speaking English, and reverted back to my native German tongue. This was my initial reaction of shock. Yet even in this state, I was able to remember that we are all spirit and that Julian too was still alive, though without a physical body. In fact, later that afternoon, we experienced his presence and spirit around the house very strongly, as we did for the next few days.

The other young man's family, however, was unable to move quickly to acceptance and support for their son because they lacked the knowledge and tools to support his transition. Their strong emotional reaction made it difficult for him because he felt guilty that he had caused his family so much distress. Over two years went by before he was fully able to accept the repercussions of his accident and let go. In comparison, Katja's son was in illumination very soon after his death and was excited about learning from teachers grouped around him.

My guides have described grief as an inability to accept what is. Grief is often experienced in waves, with periods of acceptance interspersed with periods of resistance. Gradually acceptance deepens, and peace of mind can be regained. With an understanding of how grief affects the individual who has died, our focus should be placed on acceptance, in order to work through mourning as quickly as possible.

CHAPTER FOUR: Attachment and Earth-Bound Spirits

Y EARS AGO, I HAD FRIENDS IN Plymouth, Massachusetts who lived in a large, elegant, turn-of-the-century home. During a visit there, I came in contact with an earth-bound spirit who had been the original owner. As I walked down the front stairway of the house, I literally passed through her etheric form. When this occurred, I was able to clairvoyantly perceive the house from her perspective, seeing through her eyes how it was decorated and arranged during her lifetime. What was now Henry and Shirley's living room had been her library, and what had been her living room was now a workspace for textile art.

In sharing this experience with my friends, they were excited to describe the woman who had previously lived in their house. Henry and Shirley explained that the original owner had actively participated in the construction and design of the house. It had been her dream house, a vehicle into which she poured her focus, passion, and identity.

My sense of this woman as I walked through her etheric body was that she was depressed. She was reluctant to let go of what she saw as an important piece of her identity. As she could not bring her dream house into the spiritual world, she stayed in limbo due to her strong attachment to this possession.

We decided that it was important to help this woman, for she was lonely and unhappy in her present state. We sat and meditated, called her to us, and communicated using Christian terminology that was familiar and reassuring to her. We expressed to her that she was dead, that her house was now loved and well-tended by its current owners, and that she would be much happier in the heavenly realms. We also pointed out a blue light above her, and encouraged her to walk into this light, where guardian angels would be present to comfort, guide, and protect her. Coaxing and reassurance were necessary to give her confidence to go on. As she moved towards the light, she waved good-bye and thanked us, while proceeding into expansion and liberation.

The next day, Henry and Shirley's daughter Dinah visited. We asked her what was different about her parents' home. Dinah methodically went through the entire house and concluded that we had opened all the windows and aired it out, for the house now felt fresh and full of light. We all agreed that the density and staleness were gone. The depression of this earth-bound woman had created a cloudy feeling in the house, which had affected everyone who lived there.

The presence of any individual's attitudes and emotional state affects the vibration of the immediate environment, whether the individual is in a physical body or not. When this woman experienced release from her depression, loneliness, and trapped state, the house was liberated as well. It became a more enjoyable environment for my friends.

With clairvoyant perception, I have always seen a circle of light above the head of an earth-bound spirit that appears like the entrance of a tunnel. The light can vary in color, but in most cases I've seen it as a scintillating blue. This blue light represents the spiritual qualities of expansion, openness, and the infinite. Once an individual is in contact with this light or illumination, help from guides can be received. All that is needed is for the trapped individual to look up into the light and walk towards it with a desire to be freed and comforted.

The process of liberating poltergeists, or individuals trapped in the earth vibration after death, is often very simple. It is necessary to communicate openly with them about their present circumstance, then assure them that help is available. It is also important to find the appropriate tone and words best suited to a specific individual. Occasionally, I have had to patiently soothe and encourage these entities for a significant amount of time to help penetrate the accumulated fears that are the underlying source of their problems and prevent their liberation. At other times, I have witnessed quick release and have received immediate gratitude.

In the story of the female ghost in the Plymouth house, the primary attitude that created an experience of limitation for her was her attachment to a place. The next story I describe involves a man who was attached to self-pity, an attitude he cultivated as a response to chronic disease in his physical body.

When my ex-husband and I bought our first home, we discovered that it housed an earth-bound spirit. I remember being extremely surprised when we were guided to purchase this house. The vibration of it was unattractive to me, even though its aesthetics were in harmony with my taste.

It became clear why the house felt heavy and grey when clairvoyantly we saw an elderly man in etheric form moaning and groaning in the back bedroom. He was in his pajamas, curled up on a small bed in a corner of the room. It appeared to me that his anguish had lasted for many years after his death. Although he was in a realm with no time, he was experiencing an eternal moment of misery. Similar to the story of my mother, this man continued to see himself as sick long after he had dropped his body. His inability to let go of this old image caused him to manifest illness in the after-death state.

We talked with him about death and about his circumstance, communicating that his suffering and loneliness were unnecessary, and that he no longer needed to remain stuck in this house and in pain. In this dialogue, we explained through thought that there was a light above him which was an entrance into a more expanded realm where guides existed who would help and teach him. He was not reluctant to go on, having grown tired of his unhappiness. He was able very quickly, through the use of our instructions, to move into a realm of light.

Soon afterwards, we spoke with neighbors about the history of our house. It was confirmed that an owner who had died about fifty years earlier had been ill for a very long time. There was a gravestone in the local cemetery marking the spot where his body was buried. It was ironic to me to imagine that his family and friends thought that he was resting peacefully under the ground, when he had actually been in agony in his old home, needing assistance to go on. Through our intervention, not only did he experience a liberation and an ability to continue his growth process, but we received benefits as well. It was remarkable to feel how much more comfortable and pleasant the house became after his depression was gone.

As these stories illustrate, the attitudes an individual holds in life and during the death process can contribute to a release into an expansion of light, or can cause a sense of being stuck and contracted, clinging to people, places, or old self images. A conscious or unconscious focus on fears or attachments for an extended period of time can make the process of dying difficult. When this has been the case, the actual liberation from the physical body can be experienced without a sense of liberation at all.

It is important to remember that attitudes are extremely powerful in contributing to the quality of both one's life and after-death state. Attitudes, which are the combination of thoughts and feelings, work as magnets in the spiritual realms, immediately drawing an individual to a certain location, person, or manifestation. In the spiritual dimensions, the effect of attitudes occurs instantaneously due to the absence of the element of time. The speed of the impact of thoughts and feelings in non-material realms has clearly demonstrated for me the importance of harnessing attitudinal forces for the purpose of positively affecting all circumstances of life.

Another example of aiding an earth-bound spirit took place when a woman who was renting a house locally contacted me. She was having difficulty with a ghost who was frightening her, often waking her in the middle of the night. I asked her to bring together a few friends willing to meditate with me in order to create an expansive force, through thought and focus, for the purpose of liberating the trapped individual.

Only one friend came, so the three of us sat and meditated in the living room as I called the poltergeist to us. I could see clairvoyantly an older woman who was extremely frightened. As I projected my consciousness into her, it felt as though her life had been very narrow and unfulfilled. Again I expressed the basic important message that she was dead, and that if she looked above her, there would be a light. I encouraged her to move towards this light where she would find help from guardian angels.

At first, the woman was not able to respond to my words. She appeared to be too frightened and needed reassurance. I expressed to her that she was loved and had nothing to fear, that her quality of life at present was not happy, and I emphasized the benefits of going into the light. My sense of her was that she was strongly attached to the house where she had lived, because of a deep fear of the unknown. It felt as though she had been afraid of going places and doing things before her death. These tendencies did not change once her physical body dropped.

With much encouragement, she was able to move into the light. The astonishing part of the experience for me was that as her fingertips entered into the blue light, many enlightened and compassionate guides were then able to grab her and pull her into their realm. She resembled a child who had fallen into a deep hole in the ground and was being pushed up to the many loving and helpful hands of rescuers who had been waiting patiently.

Illumined beings residing in the light of spiritual realms cannot enter into the depression and density surrounding individuals caught in the extreme level of fear and contraction experienced by earth-bound spirits. However, when individuals stuck in etheric form wish to release the past and go towards the future, they regain hope, and movement towards the light becomes possible. This process can be helped by someone in the physical body, or through attitude changes that dissolve fears and eliminate the anchoring in density. Liberation is created by an internal refusal to suffer any longer, and a shift to a positive focus.

The liberation of the frightened woman in the last story led to a chain reaction of events that demonstrates the interconnection between the material and spiritual realms. The day following this woman's release from an earth-bound state, her sister Lydia, who lived in a nursing home, made her transition into the next dimension of life. These two sisters had lived together for a long period of time and were emotionally bonded. It appeared to me that when the earth-bound sister finally let go into the light, her sister Lydia was also freed to move on.

Another interesting point regarding this story concerns the house itself, which had been on the market for some time. Though the owner of the house is skeptical of my explanation, I believe that once the ghost had been freed, and her distress eliminated from the house, its beauty and desirability became more apparent. It then sold soon afterwards.

These stories dramatically demonstrate the negative ramifications of attachments and the inability to let go. Each earth-bound spirit was caught in fear. These fears created attachments that prevented liberation after the physical body was dropped. Attachment is the emotional holding on to one point or another in the life process due to fear. This blocks a full expansive approach to living and dying. Fears can vary; people may suffer from the fear of the unknown, the fear of what other people think, or the fear of being inadequate. Whether a person is in a physical or an etheric body, fears and attachments interrupt the ability to go fully on to the next moment.

Chapter Five: Stuck in the Repetition of Trauma

*A*S CHILDREN ENTER INTO THE world, their approach to life is one of discovery and adventure. When there is a sense of discovery, life endeavors are enjoyed and opportunities are created and taken. Fear and trauma interrupt this expansive approach to life, and promote habits of narrow-mindedness and negativity. These repetitive patterns interfere with the experience of newness, curiosity, and the creative possibilities of each moment.

Psychological trauma occurs when there is

an unwanted circumstance, and an individual is not able to let go of imagery and feelings associated with the event. An internal repetition takes place in which these undesirable experiences are re-lived. Whether this occurs in the material or spiritual realms, such repetition interferes with the ability to be open to life and new learning.

Trauma can lead to a variety of undesirable outcomes. When a person is in emotional trauma in the physical realm, it can create depression or other psychological disorders which interrupt the ability to function in a happy and healthy way. In some cases, it can create a veil which blocks a person from experiencing and perceiving life in a sharp, vivid manner, and keeps the individual trapped in an emotional cloud. This results in imbalanced behavior.

If traumas are not resolved within one life, they become lodged in the soul and carried over into the next incarnation for healing and resolution. After death, when an entity goes into the light, guides and helpers teach spiritual principles and philosophy which focus specifically on an individual's unresolved traumas and fears. If attachments and blocks are extreme, it may not be possible for an individual to access the light and guidance until their attitudes change.

One consequence of fear and trauma in an after-death state is that an individual becomes earth-bound, holding on to an attitude or location. This phenomenon was discussed in the previous chapter. After death, trauma can also "trap" a person in the lowest and densest layer of the spiritual realm, often termed the lower astral plane, where little light exists.

A friend, Peter, had a near-death experience after a car accident and told me the story of what he saw in the lower astral plane. He witnessed a man who was unable to accept the fact that he had died falling off a ladder. The man who had died repeated the event over and over again in etheric form. He would climb up the ladder and fall off the ladder, climb up the ladder, and fall off the ladder. He could not let go of this event mentally or emotionally, and therefore stayed in the repetitive manifestation of his trauma.

Attitudes strongly affect life within the body and life after the body has been shed. The difference between the effect of attitudes in the material versus the spiritual worlds is the speed at which manifestation happens. In the spiritual realm, attitudes manifest at the speed of thought. If you think you are wearing a blue dress, you are wearing a blue dress. If you think you are in California, you are in California. In the physical dimension on earth, which includes time, an on-going repetition of thoughts and feelings is necessary for actual changes to transpire. Since many people hold contradictory attitudes, it can be difficult to recognize that materialization operates constantly in daily life. Nevertheless, before and after death, our thoughts and feelings have a definite impact on our overall circumstance.

Another situation Peter observed in the

lower astral realm involved a man who had been stabbed lying on top of a car. Again, this traumatic event was repeated over and over, because of an inability to let go and move on. When an individual dies violently, it can be more challenging to let go of the trauma.

The more unwanted an event is, the more difficult it is to let go and accept. My guides have taught, however, that trauma is not created by an event but the way an individual responds to it. A violent death is a difficult experience to endure without fear. The story of Jesus is an example of someone who suffered a violent death and avoided trauma by maintaining the spiritual attitude of forgiveness and remembering his infinite identity. The ability to sustain a spiritual awareness in all circumstances in life is difficult to accomplish. However, my guides teach that we are all evolving toward that attainment.

When faced with a dangerous or upsetting situation, I have been taught to use affirmations such as, "I am infinite Spirit." "I am Spirit and never alone." "I am Spirit and always safe." Through the repetition of affirmations we gradually absorb their meaning. These positive spiritual statements remind us that we are not just finite beings, and that whatever occurs within a given life in the physical world is a small and temporary part of our existence. By putting life events into a spiritual context, we cultivate spiritual attitudes such as forgiveness and compassion, which in turn help to prevent traumatic reactions.

In the after-death state, a quick mental or emotional change of focus to positive thoughts and feelings can bring an earth-bound or astrally-bound individual into the light of spiritual principles. The "light" is the emanation of spiritual oneness without the misconceptions or negative perceptions that create darkness. When individuals leave the physical realm and enter into the light, they are entering into the consciousness of all the spiritual principles, including the vibrational energy contained in love, compassion, acceptance, balance, harmony, and the experience of oneness.

Even if individuals are not focused in positivity or aligned with spiritual principles, if they are brought into the light of spiritual force, the experience is so powerful that self-realization takes place. Then, they can see themselves honestly and review their lives with clarity and without self-deception. The God-force or Light-force creates a healing, a regaining of the truth, and an alignment of the conscious self with the spiritual nature.

When a person is filled with love, light is created. If a person has love, but a small amount of hatred, there is a diminishing of that light. And when an individual is filled with hate, the light becomes darkness. So the amount of fear, regret, hatred, or jealousy an individual carries determines whether the experience of being stuck blocks access to light after death, or whether it allows enough light to penetrate so guides and lessons may be received. Therefore, it is advisable for people who have died to consciously focus on spiritual qualities so that adequate light and assistance can come to them.

Clairvoyantly, the spiritual realms appear to me like a layer cake. This description is largely compatible with the Christian concepts of heaven, hell, and purgatory, except that the layers are more complex and numerous. Another difference is that the area to which an individual goes after death is not permanent. The level an individual moves to is determined by the attitudes which are focused upon in the moment. Revelations and realizations can occur at any time, causing a movement upward into greater expansion and light.

In the material world, when someone is stuck in trauma, it is not necessarily all consuming. An emotional trauma can create the repetition of circumstances in one's life which are undesirable, but life can still go on and growth and learning can continue. If blockage of spiritual principles is predominant, however, then there can be stagnation of growth and deterioration of the physical body.

It is interesting to note that repetition both creates trauma and heals trauma. Repetition of fear-based attitudes creates and sustains trauma, and repetition of spiritually-based attitudes prevents and heals trauma. The power and impact of repetition is linked to the combination of the intensity and duration of one's attitudes.

Therefore, it is important for individuals to observe themselves to become aware of negative patterns, and to shift them by establishing the discipline and repetition of focus on spiritual qualities. By reiterating these qualities within the mind and focusing on them within the heart, a connection with spiritual principles is established without physical death occurring. Repeated attention on spiritual qualities should be the habit and foundation of one's life, while the manifestation of spiritual principles should be a very creative and individual process.

My guide has stated, *"If you focus upon fear,*

you shall manifest destruction. If you focus on the light of spiritual goodness, you shall manifest creative goodness. It is the individual choice of all of humanity, and it is within each individual's power to align with that which is positive."

CHAPTER SIX: Dispelling Negativity

*M*Y STUDENT JANICE WROTE THE following description of her experience:

I have been a student of Ellen's since 1988, integrating the spiritual principles she has received from her guides. It was the beginning of September 1994 when I received a phone call from my aunt complaining of scratches she noticed on both sides of her shoulders and back, some of which were bleeding. She was very concerned because she did not know how they got there. She asked if I would meditate on it to see if I could clarify what might be responsible for these occurrences that had now been going on for nearly six months. I knew I would be having a reading with Ellen in a few days, so I decided to ask her to look into it.

I had been aware that my aunt was still grieving and very depressed over the death of her husband, who died in September 1992. They had been married for over 30 years and shared a very close relationship. They never had children and thus having spent most of her life with him, she felt a deep loneliness after his death, despite the support she received from many family members and friends. Her loneliness no doubt fed her depression, making her more vulnerable to manipulation by an entity out of the body. This, in fact, turned out to be the case.

During my reading, Ellen focused on my request. She saw that my aunt's house was somewhat dark, partially because of a lack of windows and in part due to the presence of an entity that was lacking light. What was apparent was that my aunt's deep depression was permitting this entity entry into her *home, and allowing the manipulation of her as well. The form this manipulation took was the self-inflicted scratches during her sleep.*

I asked what we could do to remedy this problem. Ellen suggested that we do a spiritual cleansing of my aunt's house. She told me first to cleanse the entire house with sage, which I did. Then we lit candles in the kitchen. I remember reciting an affirmation that we were Spirit, Light, and Love, and wished to communicate with this entity. My aunt (who had taken several of Ellen's classes) and I began to meditate.

In my meditation, I connected with the entity and could feel it was a male vibration and rather grey. I told him that I loved him and sent him lots of light, and asked him to please stop disturbing my aunt during her sleep. I reminded him of the pain she was already in and that his disruption was only adding to it. I also reminded him that he was of the light, even though he could not feel it or demonstrate it. Immediately, I felt his presence leave. My aunt never experienced these episodes again.

I'm often hesitant to speak about the topic of negative entities, because the concept can be frightening. However, it feels important to address this subject in order to convey basic information that can protect people from distressing interactions. The term "negative entities" is not ideal, because every individual has an essential spiritual goodness. Nevertheless, it does describe a presence lacking in light and without spiritual attitudes. Negative entities are individuals who have died and are stuck in lower levels of existence in the non-physical realm. Their feelings of insignificance and inadequacy can cause them to become malicious and manipulative towards those in the physical world as a way of feeling powerful.

I first became aware of negative entities when my daughter was an infant. I was home alone in a tiny house feeling frightened and insecure about being a new mother. My fears created a susceptibility which drew in a negative presence. As I walked through a threshold within the house, I would hear a voice telling me to hurt my infant daughter. Someone else would have thought they were psychotic, but because of my clairvoyance I was able to see a dark figure trying to influence me to do harm. I affirmed out loud, "In the name of love and light and spiritual masters, be gone." As I focused on spiritual principles and deities, this negative being left. I discovered that my protection was mental and emotional positivity and an internal feeling of invincibility.

From this experience, I learned that malicious entities are attracted by fear and negative thinking. These types of interactions are more common than people realize, although they are often subtle. Without clairvoyance, people usually blame themselves for the negative thoughts and reactions that are, in fact, being instigated by a disruptive being in non-physical form. Yet whether these entities are seen and acknowledged or not, positivity is a universal protection.

My second experience with a negative entity was even more dramatic. I was in the early stage of labor with my second child when I saw clairvoyantly a dark and powerful etheric being in our dining room. His darkness and intensity scared me, and I felt vulnerable in my present state. Immediately, my spiritual guide came and comforted me. He expressed that if I saw the essential spiritual goodness in this dark presence, and felt love for him, he would have no power over me. So with all my concentration, I bore into him with my mind. I experienced the light and beauty of his spiritual essence and felt love for him and for all beings. Instantly, he was out of our house. Once again, I learned that love and light and positivity are the ultimate protection.

Fear and negativity are like an open window which allows negative entities to come in and be disruptive. While there are several techniques that can be used to disarm and deflect them, I have found the same basic principles to be essential and effective. Light dispels darkness.

Spiritual attitudes dissipate negative attitudes. Although these concepts seem simple, they can be challenging to implement in daily life. Discipline and vigilance are necessary in order to achieve consistency of positive thought and emotions.

In my counseling practice, I have found that people in extreme despair or fear are particularly susceptible to negative attack. This group includes those who have had a traumatic childhood, and therefore tend not to feel safe in the world, as well as individuals who are very self-destructive, such as alcoholics and drug-abusers. I have also found that individuals who make significant and valuable contributions to society need to take extra care to maintain a positive self-image and trust in the life process, because negative entities often enjoy making trouble and disrupting constructive work.

Positivity can be defined as an energy or a force that is created by spiritual qualities, such as love, compassion, clarity, and unity. This force of positivity is created by deep inner attitudes, rather than by superficial actions or appearances. Some people mistake positivity with pleasant or accommodating behaviors while the attitudes emanated may actually be negative and troublesome. Therefore, it is important to be honest and attentive to underlying feelings and to recognize their power and impact.

All beings are beings of light within their essential self. The negativity and darkness come from fears and feelings of inadequacy. When love and light and spiritual concepts are directed towards these individuals for personal protection, there is simultaneously a service and a comfort given to the misguided souls. This understanding actually increases positivity for all of life.

CHAPTER SEVEN: Preparation for Death

WHEN I WAS NINETEEN, I GOT A JOB as a "nurse's aid special." The process of finding this position felt guided, and marked the beginning of my ability to distinguish destined situations. I needed a job and looked in the newspaper where I found an advertisement for a nurse's aid. Fortunately, I didn't notice that the newspaper was two weeks old, because it got me to the right place at the right time. When I applied for the job, I was told it had been filled two weeks earlier, but a new position was available working with just one woman. I was given the job on the spot.

Narcissa, the woman in my care, was a ninety-two year old southern belle who had traveled and was quite refined, but had become considerably limited and frustrated due to her age. In the nursing home, she was known as a difficult, angry person who screamed at everyone. However, her anger quickly dissipated as I related to her with respect and kindness, and over the course of our time together, she became a wonderful companion.

It wasn't long before I understood that the most important aspect of my work with this lovely, frail lady was to help her through her fear of death. I began reading Emily Dickinson's poems about death to Narcissa, as a way to facilitate a discussion about the subject. As we talked about the poetry, I became aware that Narcissa often thought about death. She knew it was her time to die, but she was afraid. Her relatives often came to visit and clearly loved her very much, but I didn't hear them speaking about the challenging topic of death.

The discussion of death seemed to be part of my job. I asked Narcissa what she thought death was like. I probed her fears and then tried to reassure her that death was a beautiful phase of life. I explained that she didn't need to be afraid, that she would not be alone, and that guides and teachers would scoop her up and make her feel loved and wonderful.

As our time together progressed, her trust in me grew and she started to have significant dreams. Once she woke up yelling, "Ellen! Ellen! Now I understand your religion. It is the religion of love and light." She called me her church because I talked with her about spiritual matters.

One afternoon she dreamt that my mother had come and spoken with her about death and what it was like to make the transition. She said they had tea together. I asked her what my mother looked like and she told me that her hair was black and curly and that her eyes were blue.

This was exactly right and not easy to guess, so I knew her experience was genuine.

Narcissa made her transition on my birthday. I wasn't with her, but I had a vision of her as radiant, happy, and surrounded by beautiful golden light. She did not get stuck in fear, confusion, or negative imagery. Through conversations about the natural process of death, supporting her positive self-image at the end of her life, and explaining that she would not be alone in the after death state, Narcissa was prepared to immediately enter into light.

At the point of transition into the next dimension, focusing upon one's essential self as spirit and not as human is a fundamental image to hold for a smooth transition. When I was ten years old, I had an out-of-body experience that was so dramatic that I knew afterwards that my true identity was spirit and not human. One summer afternoon I went upstairs to my bedroom to take a rest. I'd been playing outside all day and felt very tired. I lay down on my bed, closed my eyes and the room started to spin. In a few moments my consciousness was on the ceiling, and I was looking down at my body asleep on the bed. I felt wonderful and expanded and knew then that my body was not my true self.

The belief that we are Spirit can be fostered through affirmations, such as "I am infinite Spirit" or "I am Spirit and I know who I am." At the time of death, the declaration "I am Spirit and I go into the light of oneness" is particularly helpful and can be coupled with looking up into light and expansion. This assertion works like a propelled arrow, directing an individual's consciousness out beyond limited realms. Whether the light is blue or white or green or gold doesn't matter. The variation in color is linked to the individual and the circumstance. This simple formula will consistently bring a dying soul into contact with guides and helpers.

Another story about the process of accepting and preparing for death concerns

Helen, a woman I counseled who had leukemia. I felt apprehensive about working with her because I knew Helen wanted reassurance that she would become healed. Instead, I was guided to tell her that it was her time to die. I had never said that to anyone, and I felt burdened by the responsibility. However, my guide from the spiritual realm firmly stressed that it was important that Helen know the truth. It was emphasized that the precious time she had should be spent with her young daughter in order to create a positive bond, significant memories, and alleviate regret.

Later, I learned through others that she felt I had given her hopelessness. Then I received a phone call from her daughter's babysitter who told me the rest of Helen's story. In her dying process Helen was surrounded by friends and family, all supportive while she left her body. Then she briefly returned to her physical body to tell those grouped around her what her experience was like. She described going through a dark tunnel into bright light, and that the light soothed her and felt like ecstasy. Helen also told everyone that she was going to return to earth very soon to help people work through fears about death.

About a year later Helen came to see me in spiritual form. She looked younger and healthy, but I recognized her. At that time I had a heart condition that was symptomatic, and sleepless nights were common because of chest pain, numbness, and fear. I often had heart attack symptoms and felt unable to perform simple daily tasks. It was my turn to experience the fear of dying and of traumatizing my children.

Helen appeared before me in etheric form when I was afraid and experiencing physical symptoms, and said, "It is not your time to die, so you don't need to be afraid." She also thanked me because I was the only person who told her the truth. Everyone else, she said, told her what she wanted to hear, which wasn't ultimately as helpful. She thanked and reassured me.

My spiritual guides told me that when I had counseled this woman with leukemia I had clarity and visual insight, but I lacked an emotional understanding of her suffering. My own struggle taught me empathy and compassion, and increased my appreciation of the complexity of letting go of physical life.

After that experience, I rode the roller coaster of my physical challenges for quite awhile. My heart pains and symptoms offered ideal opportunities to learn because they were dramatic, yet it wasn't my time to die. This syndrome gave me chances to practice dying every day, while working through fears and attachments. I learned to let go and trust that when it is appropriate for someone to make the transition into spirit, it is also the right time for all concerned.

After my recovery, I created a little game to help my children accept and prepare for the death of a loved one or their own eventual transition. With a door between us, I would explain that they were in one room and they were fine and I was in the next room and I was fine. I communicated to them that death is like going into another room and shutting the door. We are simply in different places, but we are all fine.

In preparing for death, it is also desirable to be current in one's life through addressing issues and problems as they arise. By keeping up to date, regrets and unfinished business are not carried over into the spiritual realm. This concept was illustrated by an experience I had one evening with a good friend's father who came in spirit to speak with me. I didn't know this man when he was alive, and when I met him in spiritual form he had been dead for over thirty years. With great sincerity, he communicated that in his life and in his death he had only one regret: that he had not expressed his love enough. Motivated by his concern for his son, he wanted me to convey his message so that his son would not make the same mistake. His visit also provided him with the opportunity to heal his own wound.

The message this man brought for his son is a universal one about the importance of not putting off significant conversations, of expressing love, and taking desired actions. Ask yourself, "If I were to die today, what regrets would I have? How can I live my life so that when my time to leave the earth arrives, I will be ready?"

Chapter Eight: A New Opportunity to Live

*I*HE OPPORTUNITY TO LIVE AFTER death is particularly meaningful and powerful when a person has not felt newness and opportunity within their physical life just completed. My father was not satisfied with how his life had turned out. He had many disappointments and felt as though his potential had not been fully realized.

He was a scientist and was afraid of dying because of his uncertainty about existence after death. My father had always hoped that my philosophy was true, but he didn't know it for himself. So when his time came to pass over, he didn't trust that he would be alright and that life would continue. Once my father died, however, his consciousness became freed from his ailing body and he immediately recognized that he was still alive. He was thrilled to discover that the learning and living process would continue. His scientific curiosity kicked in, and he wanted to understand the nature of spiritual reality just as he had devoted his life to studying the nature of physical reality. His enthusiasm for this next learning stage was so great that very quickly my father was able to drop old burdens and hurts that had kept him unhappy when he was alive. He truly emanated the attitude of, "Oh boy, a new opportunity to live!"

I was surprised that my father immediately embraced his new circumstance with such enthusiasm because he had carried deep discouragement and unhappiness for so much of his life. This experience showed me that change and a fulfilled inner life is only an attitude away. It also emphasized the power of curiosity as a force to propel growth. A love of learning supports and promotes optimism and the feeling of new possibilities.

I've connected with many of my clients' loved ones who have died and have observed the ease or difficulty of their transition. I have found that individuals who are excited about new experiences rather than afraid of the unknown are much more likely to be renewed and rejuvenated quickly in the after-death state.

Just recently I did a session for a man who asked me to look into his father who had died ten years earlier. By focusing on his name I was able to sense and see that he was still stuck and unhappy. His life had been one of continual hard work as a farmer. He didn't particularly enjoy his role or his daily life, and had developed the feeling that life was a burden. This attitude was sustained for a long period of time, and when his liberation from the body came, he brought his state of mind with him into the next dimension of life. Even though he was given a new opportunity, he didn't take it, but stayed focused on the past and the emotional feelings of heaviness. His life had a quality of sameness, without the variety of newness and change.

I cannot emphasize enough the significance of focusing on the ever-changing experience of being alive. No day is ever the same. No person is ever the same. No view is ever exactly the same. Through focusing on the nuances and changes in evolution, the feeling of new opportunities for creativity, learning, and development are abundant.

When my dear friend Tom died at the age of 82 while having a cup of coffee with friends in a New Zealand café, I was initially saddened. I knew his endearing idiosyncrasies would no longer be a part of my present life. When I tuned into him and felt his anger and disappointment at his passing, I realized that I needed to snap out of my grief, and focus on helping him move to a positive acceptance of his new chapter.

Tom was a very talented healer and always seemed to have a big agenda. He wanted to heal and help masses of people and he longed for a personal, loving, fulfilling life. When he realized he was dead, he felt that both these desires were cut short. He felt cheated by spirit, because he didn't feel finished with his life.

I talked to Tom and encouraged others who knew him to send light and love and communicate to him that he was very appreciated for his healing gifts, and for his quirky and delightful personality. It took about two weeks for him to accept and embrace his new situation. Since then he has gone on, focused on learning and enjoying the miracle of the spiritual, loving force. I no longer feel regret or anger from him, because this new opportunity, when embraced, is deeply satisfying.

The following is a story written by a student, Paula, who experienced an out-of-body dream where she reconnected with her father in the spiritual realm. There, she saw him as youthful, rejuvenated, and ready to take on a new chance for a better life.

My father died of pneumonia September 3, 1997 at the age 89. For most of my life, he and I were not close. He was an alcoholic who was unconscious about spirit, but he was someone who provided for his four children in the only way he knew how. Unfortunately, because of his alcoholism my childhood was painful for me and we were deprived in many ways – economically, culturally, and emotionally. As a result, there were unresolved resentments between us which didn't get addressed until he became ill.

My father had a stroke in 1995, and until that time, I was unable to see his spirit and to forgive him. During the three years he was sick, we spent many hours together and I managed to communicate some of my feelings to him. I also came to feel that he loved me, despite his inability to express it in words, but I was never really sure.

My dad died unexpectedly, and I was unable to

say good-bye. I knew because of what I had experienced in Ellen's classes that death was a transition from one stage of existence to another. I also knew that once he dropped his physical body, he would no longer be in pain, and I found that thought comforting. However, when he died I did not have an opportunity to say good-bye and I felt deeply sad.

Six months after my father passed away, he appeared to me in a dream that was vividly real. It felt completely different from any dream I had ever had. I saw my father sitting down on a bleacher with his head turned towards me. I remember thinking how wonderful he looked, radiant and younger than I'd ever seen him look before. I also noticed that he had all his teeth, because he'd worn dentures since I was a child. I knew it was my dad for certain when I saw that he was wearing a favorite bow tie he owned when I was 11 years old.

He smiled at me with such peace in his eyes, and told me that he understood so much more than he had ever understood while he was in the body. He said that he was sorry that he hadn't been a very good father, and told me that he loved me. He said to tell my sister and brother that he loved them very much, and asked me to take care of my sister, because he had not taken care of her when he was alive. He told me that she would need my support over the next few years, and she has.

Just before my dad left, he looked at me directly and smiled, and then disappeared before my eyes. Following this experience, I felt as though any attachment to regret was gone, and since that time, I'm able to think about my father without feeling excessively emotional, which I had previous to this contact. Although the experience still moves me emotionally, I now feel free to go on with my life just as my dad is free to move on with his.

In this account, I love the fact that Paula's father was wearing his favorite bow tie. For when individuals in etheric form have experienced rejuvenation and rebirth, they take on the appearance of their favorite self-image. People often appear in images depicting their late 20s or early 30s, a time when many feel young and vital, and yet mature. A common exception to this seems to be wise and profound teachers who choose to appear old and venerable.

I was also moved by the fact that the healing power of the light and the outer spiritual realms allowed this man to find peace, clarity, and forgiveness, even though he had been an alcoholic who struggled and suffered a great deal in his life. The experience of passing into the light of the spiritual realm has the power to wash away hurts, regrets, and ignorance. Everyone, no matter what they have endured or suffered within a given life, will ultimately become renewed and cleansed.

CHAPTER NINE: The Practice of Letting Go

*W*HEN YOU PERCEIVE NATURE, YOU observe that everything is in a constant state of change. Life flows from one moment to the next and from one experience to the next. Therefore, if people want to experience harmony and well-being with life, they must learn to function like the natural world. People have choice to be in harmony with life or not, while a flower just is. The process and practice of letting go of attachments allows life to move freely from one experience to the next without becoming caught in past memories or feelings.

When the process of letting go does not happen easily, it can be developed through intention, focus, and practice. Originally I started this training so that if I had to let go of my home or my children or my life, I could do so without becoming traumatized. I began the practice of letting go of my attachments during my daily three mile walks. I would focus on one possession, person, or place at a time. As I walked, I would visually and literally pull fears and attachments out of me while affirming, "I let go, I let go, I let go." If I discovered a feeling of resistance, then I knew this was an area that required more work. I aspired to be able to let go of everything.

To my surprise, as I let my attachments go, my perceptions sharpened, I felt more pleasure in daily living, and my feelings of love intensified. It was inspiring to me that this simple practice was effective in creating a sense of expansion and well-being. My guides say that attachment contains the fear of loss and when the fear is released happiness and clarity are increased. An aspiration for a certain situation or relationship can exist without fear.

Since that time, I have taught many people to practice letting go of their attachments through a series of exercises similar to the ones I first did while walking. This discipline allows people to experience for themselves what it feels like to let go of fears associated with particular people, places, and things, and to gather greater insight into these personal relationships. These practices can be done at any time, although they are most effective when used during deep inner stillness and concentration. What brings these exercises to a successful conclusion is the ability to hold a focus, which is why they are essentially meditative practices.

Try this exercise. Mentally choose a material possession. It may be a favorite article of clothing, something passed down through the family, or an expensive piece of jewelry. Now imagine your possession going up into light, and at the same time affirm, "I let go. I let go. I let go." Watch your feelings and reactions as you let the item go. Is there a release and sense of freedom, or is there a pull? Is it hard to let it go? And if it is difficult, what attitude is needed in order to create a release? In one circumstance, it may be necessary to focus on the attitude of trust, while another may require acceptance or patience.

This is not a thinking process. If you are analytical or do this exercise from a mental or intellectual level, it becomes difficult. What is effective is to repeatedly affirm the concept of letting go, while focusing on the image of what you are releasing. Through focus, you can observe what feelings come up and what images change.

The practice of letting go of a thing generates a variety of different responses. Some people feel free and unburdened, while others continue to experience the fear of loss and are only partially able to let go. Although the exercise outlined above is quite simple, the key to its success lies in repeating it as often as necessary until letting go is achieved. I have found in my work that when people completely let go of their attachments to material things, their appropriate uses and roles become apparent, appreciation is increased, and expansion is experienced.

Materialism is the valuing of material things above spiritual principles. When we let go, possessions are used in harmony with spiritual attitudes. This may take on the form of generosity, order, appreciation, or creativity. With this awareness, objects are seen as creative expressions and practical gifts that are temporarily in our care.

One day I went running and left my favorite hat on the stone wall outside my house. When I returned I discovered the neighbor's dog had chewed it to bits. I felt terrible. In all seasons but summer this hat was like an appendage to my head. Boy, was I attached to this silly little thing – I tried to let go of my attachment, but I felt regret. Whenever I saw anyone wearing a hat, I missed mine. I tried buying other hats that were similar, but none of them felt as right.

I practiced letting go for a long time before I stopped feeling regret that my treasured hat had been destroyed by the neighbor's dog. When emotionally I accepted this fact completely, I stumbled on a store in New York City that had a dozen hats just like mine. I bought a new one, but now I enjoy it without attachment.

Attachments, whether to a person, place, thing, or idea, can cause emotional imbalances that interrupt inner peace, clarity, and manifestation. The story of my hat illustrates an important concept – when you let go of anything and it's meant to be yours, it will come back. When fears and attachments are released, blocks are eliminated and life is able to flow. This allows what is meant to be to manifest.

I once had a client that experienced this concept in a relationship. Leslie struggled with letting go of an intimate relationship that had ended. Years went by before she stopped being in turmoil. When finally she fully accepted the situation, amazingly the man from her past called. He was ready to renew the relationship.

People are often afraid to let go because of the confusion about what it actually means. Too often it is believed that letting go means giving up hope. On the contrary it signifies trusting life. The probability of manifesting our desires is much greater when we trust rather than fear.

Try letting go of a person in your life. Choose someone important to you. Imagine this person going into light and again affirm, "I let go. I let go. I let go." Be aware of what you feel. Increased love? Fear of loss? If you still experience fear, then the process of letting go is not complete and should be practiced more.

If it is difficult to do this exercise, it may be that fear is affecting the quality of your relationship. Too many relationships are based on the fear of being alone or the fear of not feeling safe. Through the practice of letting go, these relationships can be improved and made healthier. When a person is released easily into light, there's a feeling of wholeness and the recognition that each individual can be complete and strong in herself or himself. Relationships need not be based in neediness, but instead in love, creativity, and sharing.

In relationships, attachments and fears are often quite layered and complicated. Therefore, patience, practice, and repetition are required for this exercise to be effective. What occurs in this practice is the release of fear and limitation, not a loss of the love or the bond. Also, when letting go is done deeply, greater clarity about the appropriate nature of the relationship is revealed.

Too often people in the material world do not perceive their spiritual identity as who they truly are. They become attached to things, people, and concepts in order to create a sense of identity. These perceptions are not based in spiritual clarity. Therefore, fulfillment escapes them and anxiety results. When attachments are released, what is left to feel and to focus upon is essence. Essence is filled with spiritual qualities, such as joy in existence and compassion for others. These deep spiritual feelings are thoroughly satisfying. All of the experiences and interactions of daily life are enhanced when attachments are dissipated.

Along with people and things, I ask students to practice letting go of concepts.

For example, focus on the concept, "All single mothers struggle." Then let go of this idea, putting it into the light while affirming, "I let go, I let go, I let go," as was done in the previous exercises. In my experience and that of many of my students, this concept just dissolves because it is not universally true. However, when I state "I am Spirit, infinite Spirit," and I put that concept in the light and affirm, "I let go, I let go, I let go," I then feel as though I embody the concept, and instead of thinking about it, I experience it in my being. When a concept is true, it stays with you and expands as you let it go. When a concept is false, it breaks up and falls away.

Having practiced this letting go exercise with many different ideas and images, I have found it to be useful in revealing what is universal and clear as well as thinking that is limited and unproductive. Letting go works like a magnifying glass and is a wonderful technique for discovering which concepts or attitudes are appropriate and which should be released.

As you affirm letting go, understanding grows and discernment develops. This allows the clarity needed for attuned action to emerge. Letting go is synonymous with acceptance of what is, and from that state of inner stillness clarity comes naturally. It then becomes easier to identify priorities and the appropriate types of relationships to have with people, things, and concepts.

At the time of death, the letting go process is unavoidable. Individuals must relinquish their material possessions and physical relationships, since the ability to interact through the physical senses is no longer possible. When the habit of letting go of attachments is cultivated regularly in material life, then the inevitable letting go process at the time of death is not overwhelming, but quite natural. Simultaneously, this preparation fosters a better quality of life in the human form.

My guides often state that when you prepare for death, then you really live. The process of releasing fears with mental and emotional imagery, coupled with positive, affirmative thoughts improves the value and enjoyment of living, as well as the acceptance and the adventure of dying.

When letting go is achieved, wholeness is experienced. When wholeness is affirmed, letting go is achieved. Here is a quote emphasizing this point from a guide who wishes to contribute to the topic:

It is my desire to share with you the feeling of wholeness. It is my desire to share with you the feeling of no insecurity. For within your very self is that which is secure. When you sit in the wholeness of your being, you do not need to cling to others, circumstances, or concepts. You can allow life to unfold as you maintain the dignity and integrity of your nature in full expression, interaction, and creativity. Therefore, as you let go of fear and limitation, you open yourself to full involvement, full caring, and full potential. Open yourselves now in letting go of limitation, affirming that you are unlimited in your nature, and therefore free. As you move through your lives of time schedules, money constraints, and demands that are placed upon you within your human existence, maintain your attitude of unlimited identity. As you move through the world of limitation, couple that experience with the attitude of infinite source. You shall find that the movement and the interaction shall be changed. For as your identity is acknowledged in the spirit, the light and emanation coming off of you shall impact the vibrational interaction and the daily tasks. Practice, for it is the joy of daily tasks that bring you into the enlightenment of the self.

Happiness is sustained with the ability to trust and be present in the learning of the moment. This applies universally whether the learning and experiences are within the physical or spiritual realm.

Chapter Ten: Conclusion

*A*S I TRACE PEOPLE THROUGH THEIR incarnations, watching them move back and forth between the material and spiritual realms, I see that there is a tremendous amount of repetition. I observe people making the same errors over and over again, due to their focus on attitudes and actions that are not based in spiritual qualities. This creates enormous suffering. However, not at any time do my guides get discouraged or waiver from their belief that everyone shall be successful in the actualization of their spiritual nature, and that all souls shall eventually be drawn into light.

Once when I was sitting in a restaurant waiting for a friend, I looked out the window and saw two disheveled, unhappy-looking people sitting on a park bench. I asked my guide, "How are these people going to find their way and actualize their spiritual nature? I am working so diligently and consciously at this process, and they appear so much more handicapped."

Suddenly, I was given a vision of angelic beings in the sky heralding all of humanity into the light. The image reminded me of a medieval painting. In it, masses of people formed a spiral of interconnectedness. As each person moved into light and positivity, they drew all of humanity with them, for they were all linked. No one was separate or isolated. I realized in that moment that when anyone actualizes spiritual qualities all people are helped and supported in their spiritual journey.

As the vision faded, my attention once again returned to the two people on the park bench. This time, I saw them as part of the oneness and understood that they would be helped by anyone who focused on the manifestation of spiritual qualities.

A few days after these last paragraphs were written Martha Miller, who helped me edit this book, became very ill. The ovarian cancer she fought for eleven years overtook her. In three months Martha passed into the spiritual realm. This book served as a practical tool to help her in a time of need.

Death is all around us. We are exposed to death in national and world news, and more personally with friends and family members. We will all die and everyone we know and love will die. We must all face this natural part of life. It does not need to be frightening. Death is a wonderful continuation of the life process. Relationships, enjoyment, and development all continue in other realms. And then eventually through reincarnation we return to the physical world.

Although clairvoyance is often met with skepticism, it is through this gift that I can speak with confidence and sincerity that death should not be feared, but embraced as a new and interesting chapter of life. My hope is that this book will provide tools and comfort about this universally shared experience.

Acknowledgements

ANY IMPORTANT PROJECT IS ALWAYS A group effort – this book is no exception. Ken Blanchard's enthusiasm got me writing. The Marion Foundation encouraged this project. Rev. Barbara Nielsen and Janice Scangas provided support and friendship, while Jill Petty gave editorial assistance. Paula Vincent-Cowan and Joan Linden tirelessly attended to a magnitude of details. And my students and clients through the years have contributed by teaching me about the integration between the material world and spiritual realms.

Book Design: Joan Linden
Illustrations: Laszlo Kubinyi
Digital Effects: Art Torres
Photograph: Ellen Augarten